Plates, Quakes, and Glowing Magma

Written by
Laura Appleton-Smith
and Susan Blackaby

Illustrated by
Greg Harris

Laura Appleton-Smith holds a degree in English from Middlebury College. Laura is a primary school teacher who has combined her talents in creative writing with her experience in early childhood education to create *Books to Remember*.

Susan Blackaby has worked in educational publishing for over 30 years. In addition to her writing curriculum, she is the author of *Rembrandt's Hat* (Houghton Mifflin, 2002); *Cleopatra: Egypt's Last and Greatest Queen* (Sterling, 2009); *Nest, Nook, and Cranny* (Charlesbridge, 2010), winner of the 2011 Lion and the Unicorn Award for Excellence in North American Poetry; and *Brownie Groundhog and the February Fox* (Sterling, 2011). She lives in Portland, Oregon.

Greg Harris started out in advertising, working on local and national accounts for various agencies and studios before forming his own ad agency. From there, Greg expanded to commercial, children's, and educational illustration. This is his first book with Flyleaf Publishing.

Text copyright © 2013 Laura Appleton-Smith and Susan Blackaby
Illustration copyright © 2013 Greg Harris

All Rights Reserved
No part of this book may be reproduced or transmitted in any form or by any means, electronic, mechanical, photocopying, recording, or otherwise, without prior written permission from the publisher.
For information, contact Flyleaf Publishing.

A Book to Remember™
Published by Flyleaf Publishing
Post Office Box 287, Lyme, NH 03768

For orders or information, contact us at **(800) 449-7006**.
Please visit our website at **www.flyleafpublishing.com**

Eighth Edition 2/20
Library of Congress Control Number: 2013957845
Soft cover ISBN-13: 978-1-60541-154-5
Printed and bound in the USA at Worzalla Publishing, Stevens Point, WI.

*For my friend Laura, integral in the production of this book
and a wonderful design partner for many years.
I am so fortunate to be able to work with you.*

Woof.

LAS

To the Red-tailed Readers

SB

Chapter 1
The Earth's Crust

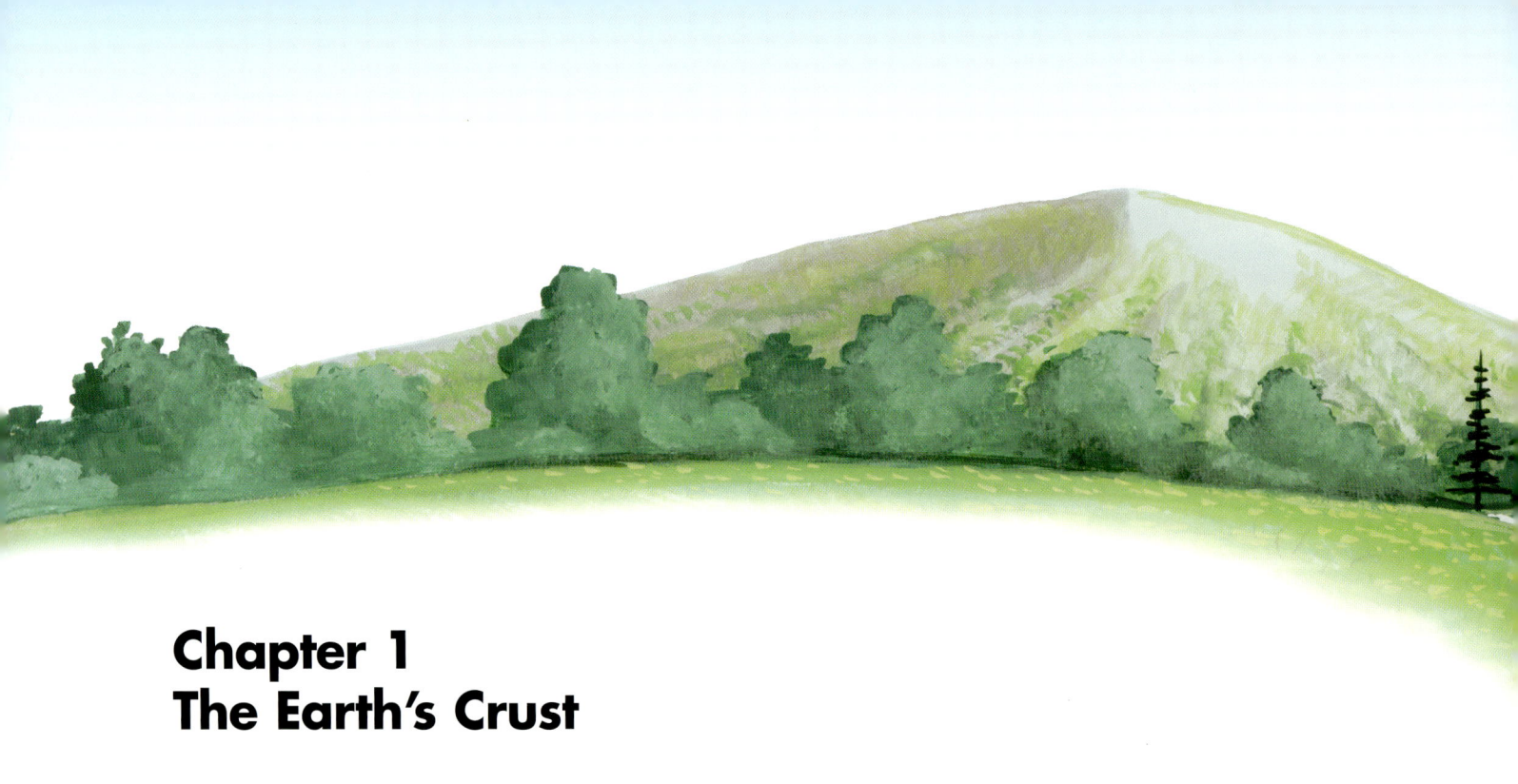

When you look at the Earth, you can see that it has water on it, and it has land with grass and plants on it.

The Earth

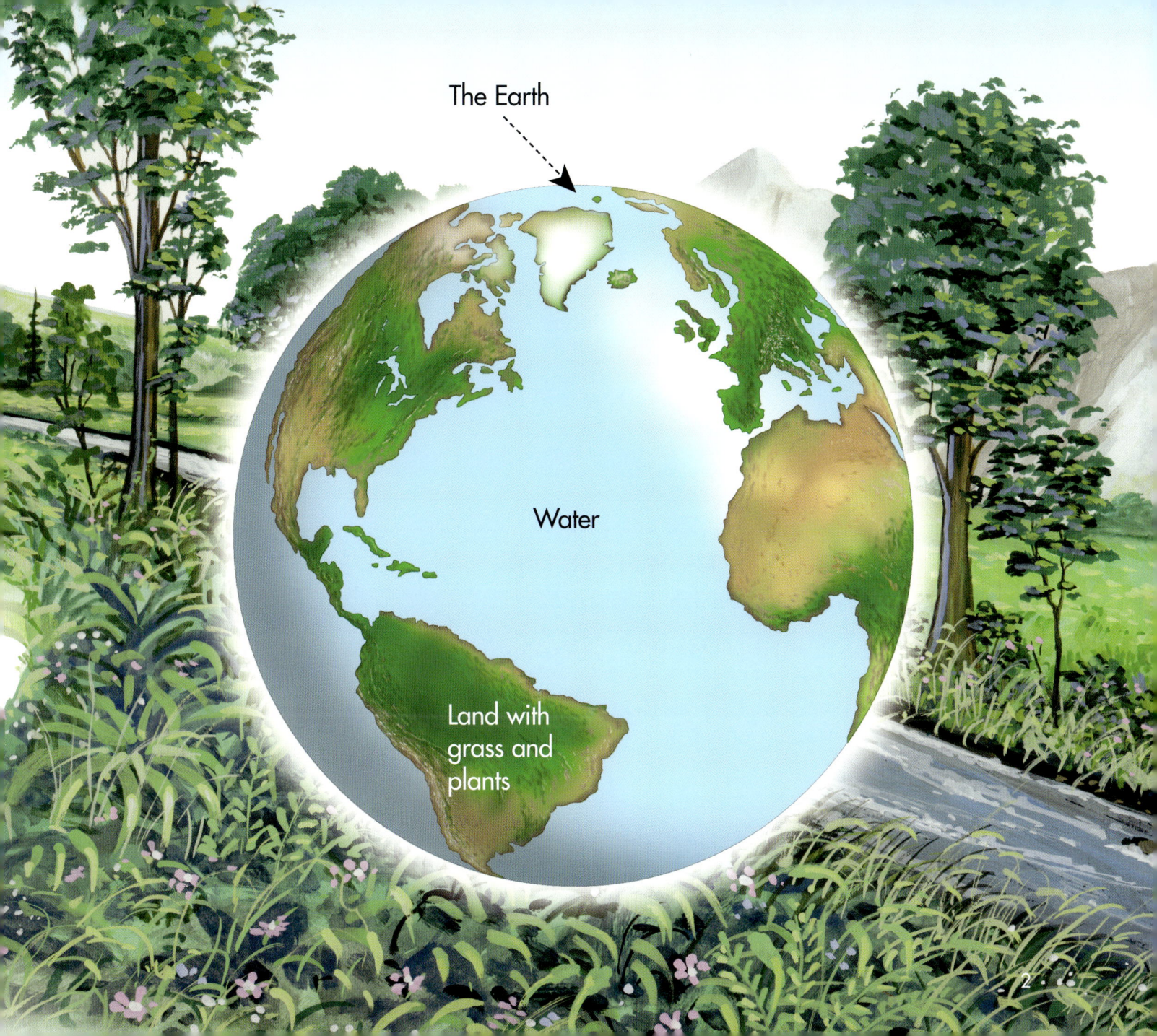

Water

Land with grass and plants

But did you know that under the land and grass and plants,
and even under the water, there is a thick layer of dirt and stones
that goes around the whole Earth?

This rocky layer that coats the Earth is called the Earth's *crust*.

If we could cut out a big wedge of the Earth and look inside,
we would see the layer of the Earth's crust under the land and water.

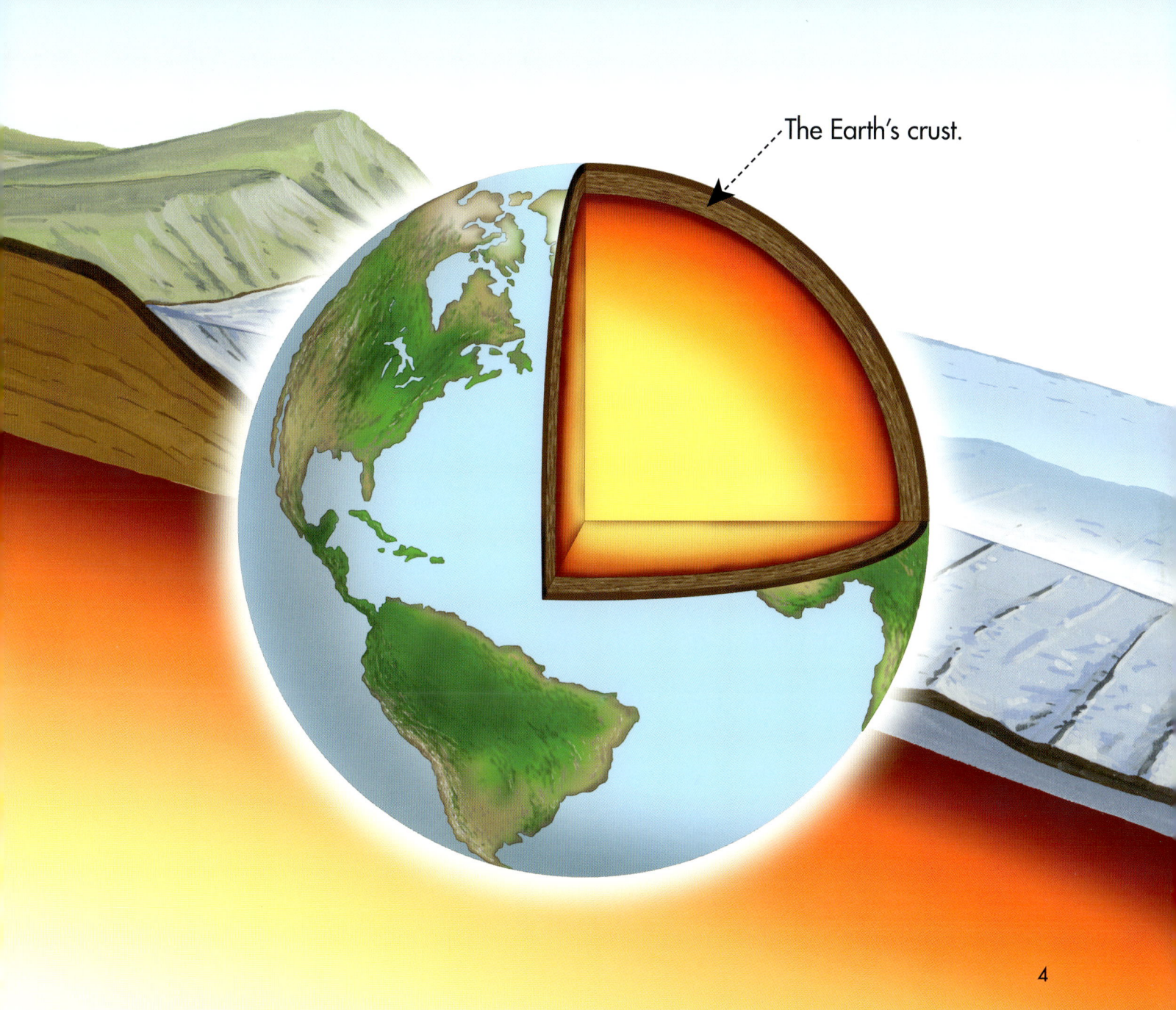

The Earth's crust.

The Earth's Plates

The Earth's crust is not one solid layer.

You can see that the Earth's crust has big cracks in it. The cracks split the crust into very big chunks. These big chunks of the Earth's crust are called *plates*.

If we make our globe flat, so it is like a map, it is possible to see some of the big plates and the cracks that go around each one.

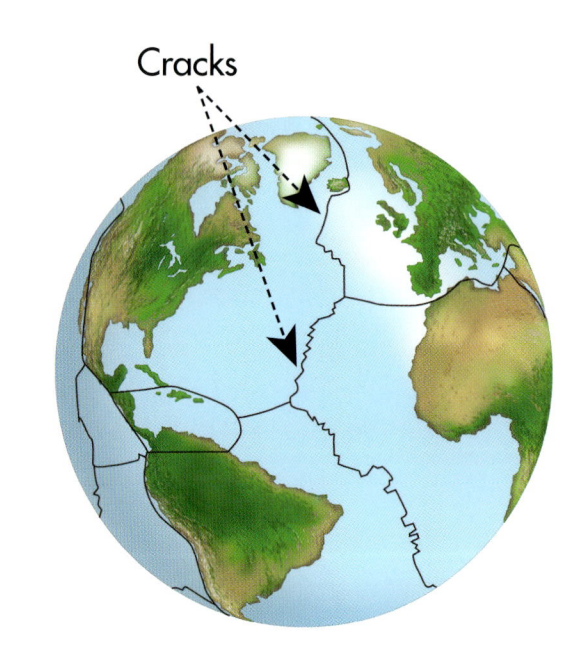

Cracks

This big chunk of the Earth's crust with cracks all around it is called a *plate*. Can you see more plates on this map?

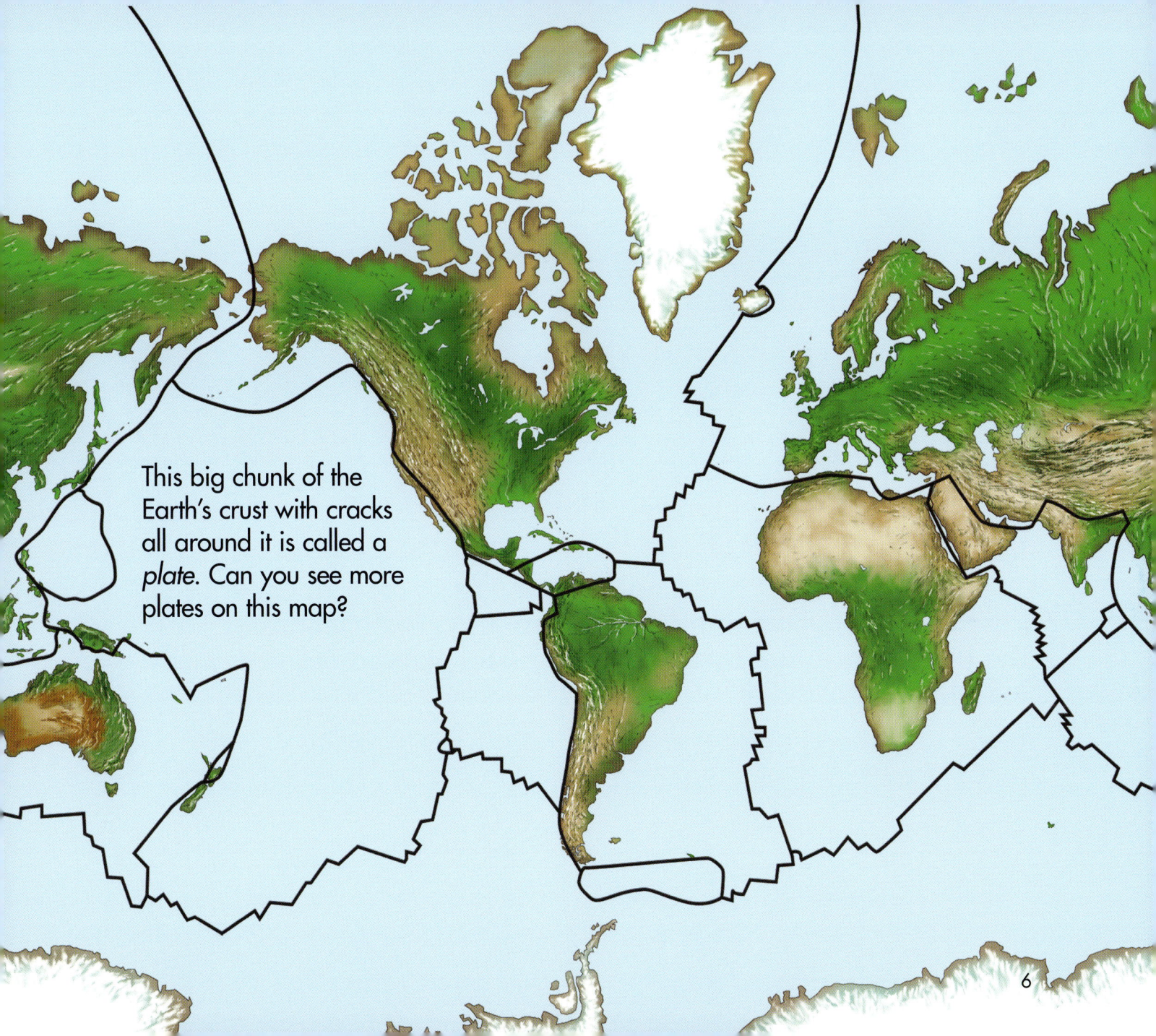

Floating Plates?

Go outside and jump up and down.

Think about the dirt and stones of the Earth's crust under your feet. Think about the fact that you are jumping on a big chunk of the Earth's crust that is called a plate. The plate under your feet feels solid, right?

What would you think if you were told that the plate you are standing on is floating?

8

Chapter 2
Glowing Magma

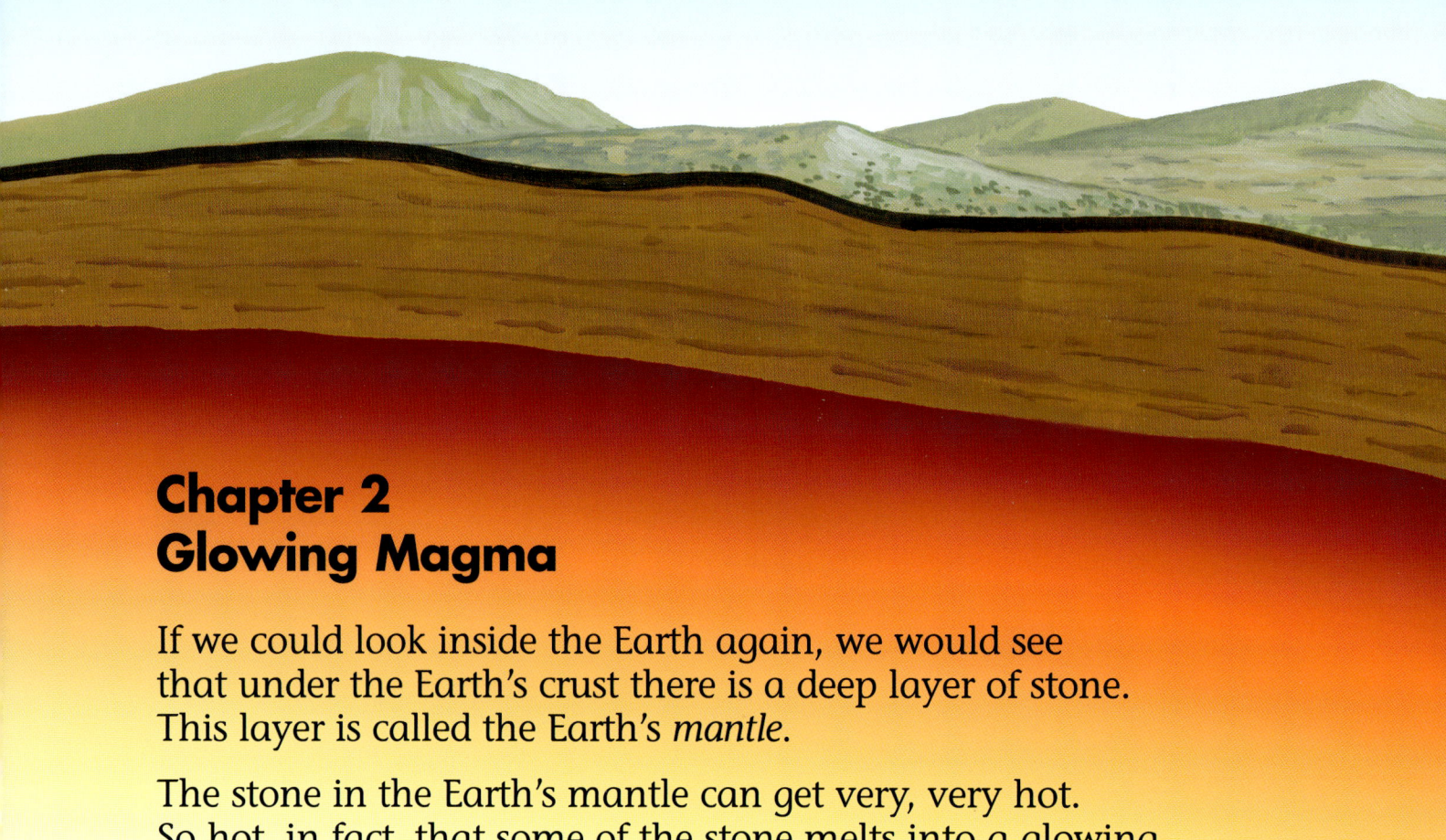

If we could look inside the Earth again, we would see that under the Earth's crust there is a deep layer of stone. This layer is called the Earth's *mantle*.

The stone in the Earth's mantle can get very, very hot. So hot, in fact, that some of the stone melts into a glowing liquid rock called *magma*. Magma is not a runny liquid, like water. It is a thick liquid, like cake batter.

Crust

Mantle

10

Now we know that the big chunks of the Earth's crust float on a layer of glowing melted rock. In other words, Earth's plates float on magma!

12

Chapter 3
Earthquakes

Because the Earth's plates float, they can move. The plates are so big that most of the time you cannot feel them moving. In fact, most of the time, you can't tell you are on a plate at all, unless you are close to the edge.

At the edge, where two plates meet, the land can shake. When the land suddenly shakes because of plates moving, it is called an *earthquake*.

If we could cut big blocks of the Earth's crust and look at them, we would see the crust moving when an earthquake happened.

14

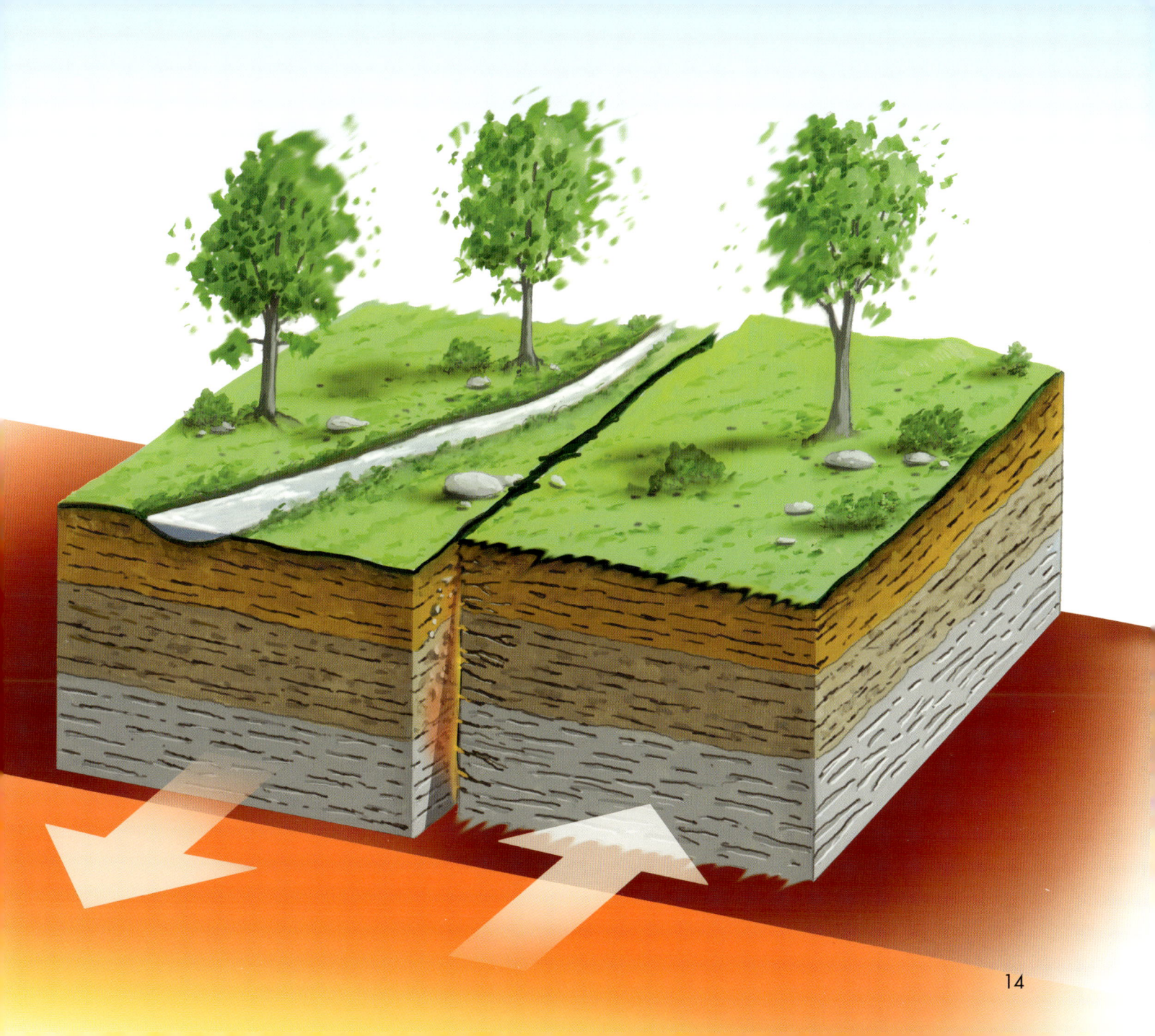

When Do Earthquakes Happen?

Some earthquakes happen when one plate slowly bumps into or slides up or down past another plate.

Some earthquakes happen when two plates slowly float away from each other and the gap between the plates gets bigger.

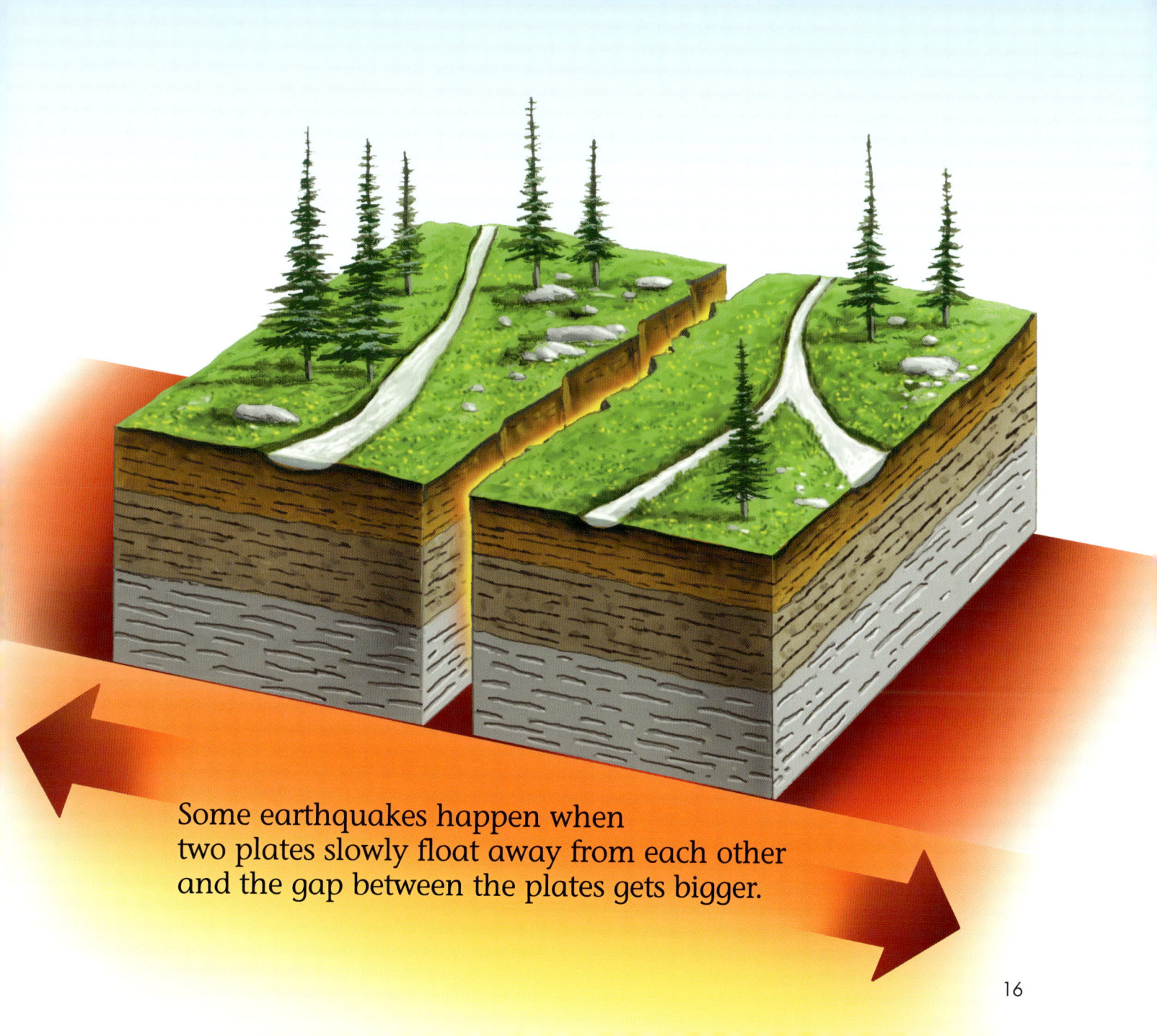

Quakes Big and Small

Did you know that quakes happen all the time?

Many quakes are so small you cannot feel them.
But big quakes can happen when plates get stuck as one plate is sliding past the other. When the plates come unstuck, the Earth's crust shakes very suddenly. This is an earthquake you can feel!

When a big earthquake happens, stones can tumble from cliffs, landslides can rumble down steep slopes, and cracks can split the Earth's crust.

18

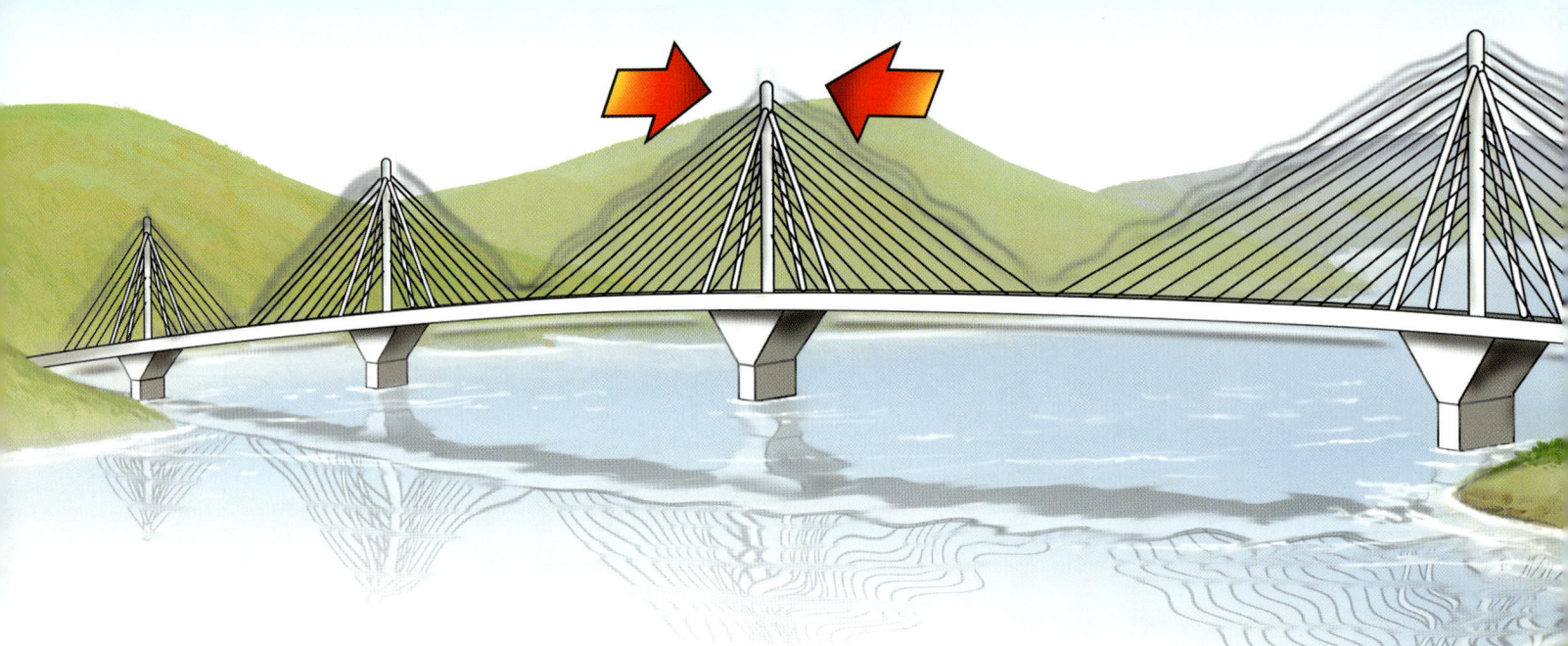

Earthquake Zones

The places on the Earth's crust where plates meet and the Earth can shake are called *earthquake zones*.

People who live in earthquake zones need to construct strong buildings, roads, bridges, and homes. These structures need to rock and bend as the Earth shakes, but not crumble or fall down in a quake. This helps to keep people who live in earthquake zones safe.

20

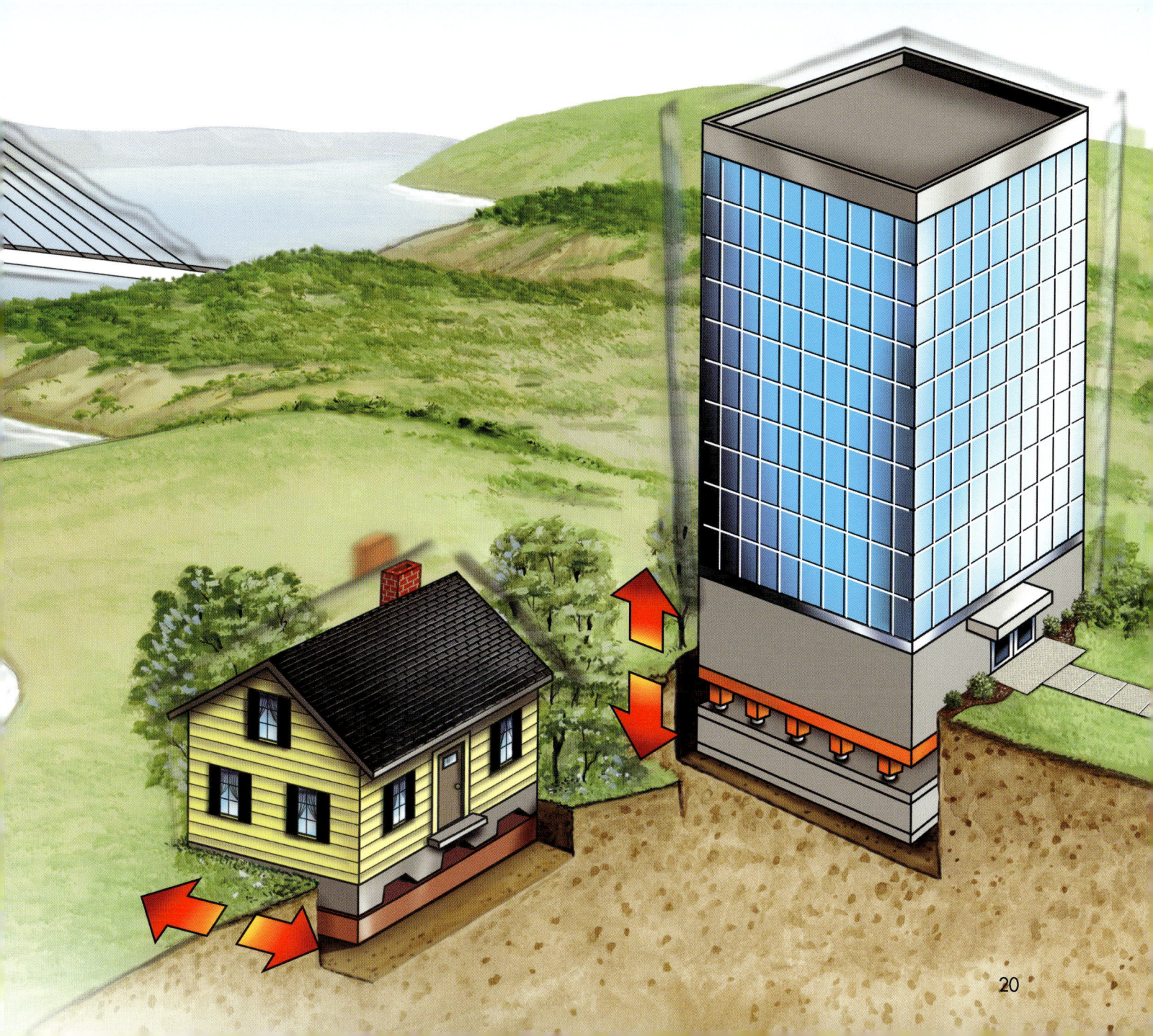

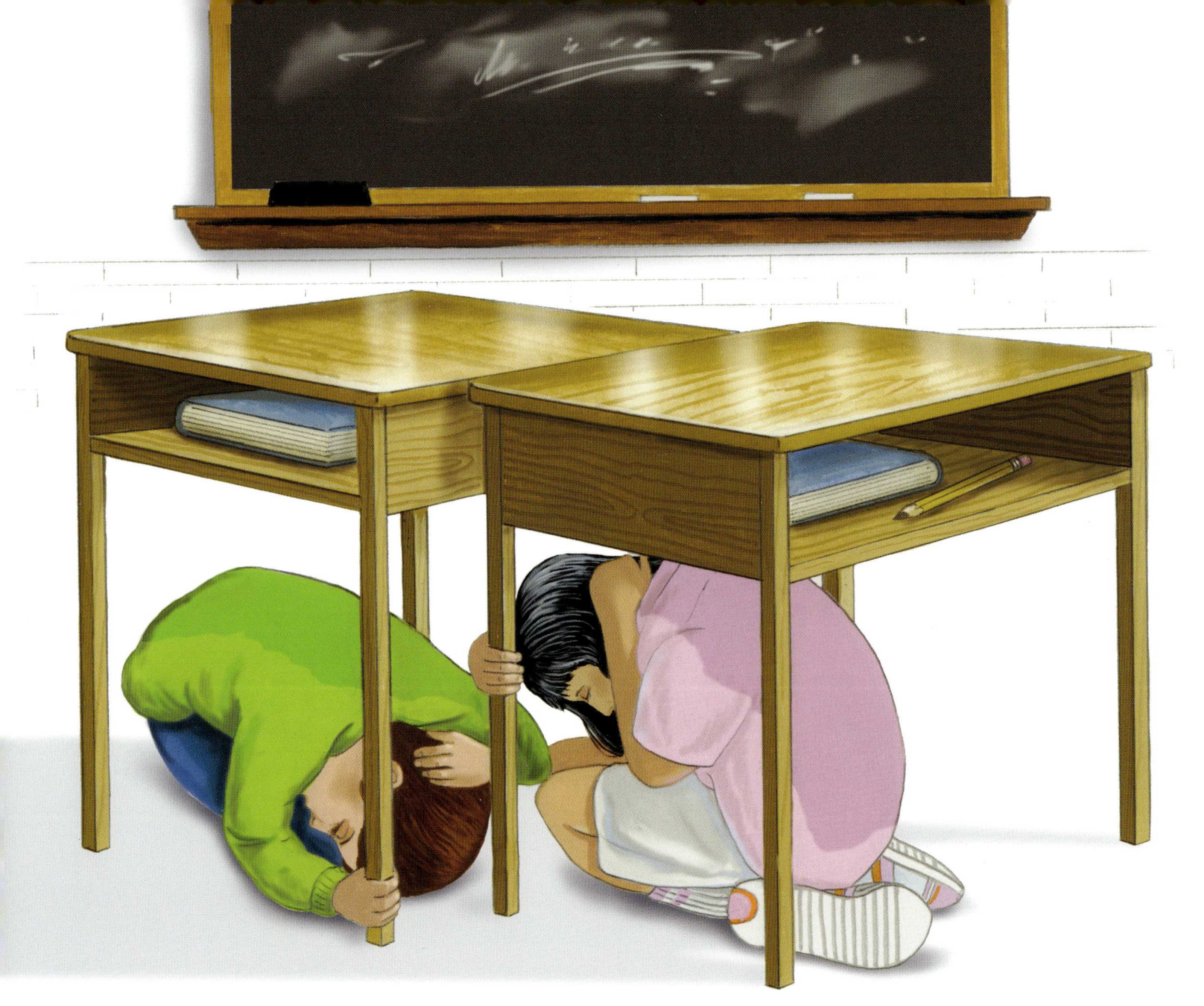

Safety in a Quake

People who live in earthquake zones need to know what to do if a quake happens. We cannot stop earthquakes from happening, but we can understand how to cope with them and keep as safe as possible.

- Drop down low. Get under a desk or table for shelter.

- Protect your head with your arms and elbows and keep your hands next to your neck (unless you need to hold on to the legs of your shelter to keep under it).

- Hold still until the shaking stops.

- After all of the shaking stops, an adult should take children to a safe spot.

Crust   Plates   Mantle

Earthquake

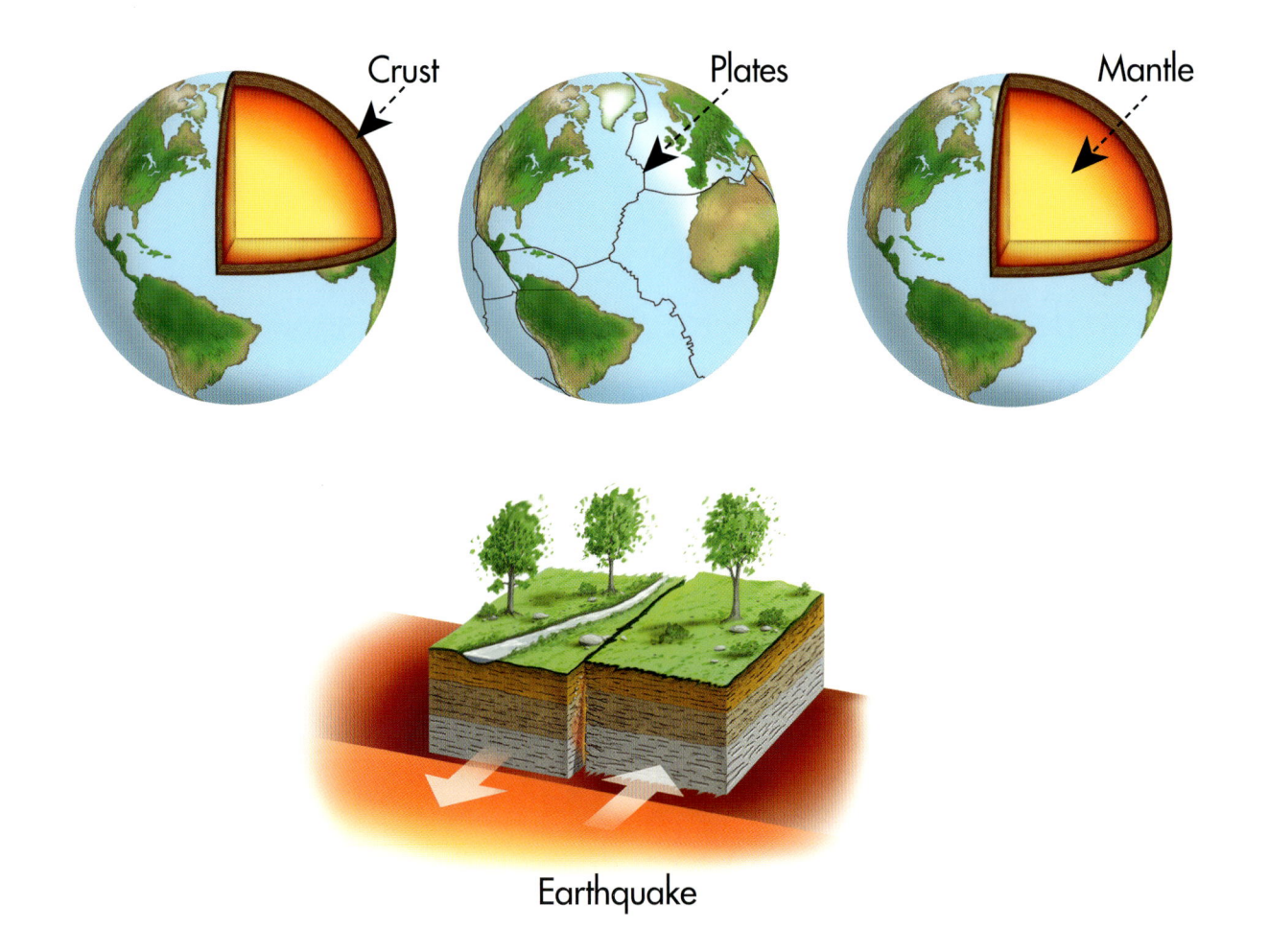

Now you know about the Earth's crust, the Earth's plates, the Earth's mantle, earthquakes, and how to keep safe in a quake. Isn't that great?

Keeping safe

Prerequisite Skills
Single consonants and short vowels
Final double consonants **ff**, **gg**, **ll**, **nn**, **ss**, **tt**, **zz**
Consonant /k/ **ck**
Consonant /j/ **g**, **dge**
Consonant /s/ **c**
/ng/ **n[k]**
Consonant digraphs /ng/ **ng**, /th/ **th**, /hw/ **wh**
Consonant digraphs /ch/ **ch**, **tch**, /sh/ **sh**, /f/ **ph**
Schwa /ə/ **a**, **e**, **i**, **o**, **u**
Long /ā/ **a_e**
Long /ē/ **e_e**, **ee**, **y**
Long /ī/ **i_e**, **igh**
Long /ō/ **o_e**
Long /ū/, /o͞o/ **u_e**
r-Controlled /ar/ **ar**
r-Controlled /or/ **or**
r-Controlled /ûr/ **er**, **ir**, **ur**, **ear**, **or**, **[w]or**
/ô/ **al**, **all**
/ul/ **le**
/d/ or /t/ **–ed**

Target Letter-Sound Correspondence

Long /ō/ sound spelled **oa**

coats	floating
float	roads

Target Letter-Sound Correspondence

Long /ō/ sound spelled **ow**

elbows	low
glowing	slowly

Target Letter-Sound Correspondence

Long /ō/ sound spelled **o_e**

close	slopes
cope	stone
globe	stones
homes	zones

High-Frequency Puzzle Words

about	more
again	most
another	now
are	of
around	one
away	other
because	our
between	out
come	people
could	right
do	should
down	so
each	some
even	there
from	they
go	to
goes	two
great	we
hold	were
how	what
into	where
know	who
live	would
look	you
many	your

Story Puzzle Words	Decodable Words			
buildings	1	construct	happens	not	still
head	2	cracks	has	on	stop
layer	3	crumble	helps	or	stops
move	a	crust	hot	past	strong
moving	adult	cut	if	places	stuck
outside	after	deep	in	plants	suddenly
protect	all	desk	inside	plate	take
structures	an	did	is	plates	tell
table	and	dirt	isn't	possible	that
told	arms	drop	it	quake	the
whole	as	Earth	jump	quakes	them
	at	Earth's	jumping	rock	these
	batter	earthquake	keep	rocky	thick
	bend	earthquakes	keeping	rumble	think
	big	edge	land	runny	this
	bigger	fact	landslides	safe	time
	blocks	fall	legs	safety	tumble
	bridges	feel	like	see	under
	bumps	feels	liquid	shake	understand
	but	feet	made	shakes	unless
	cake	flat	magma	shaking	unstuck
	called	for	make	shelter	until
	can	gap	mantle	slides	up
	can't	get	map	sliding	very
	cannot	gets	meet	small	water
	chapter	grass	melted	solid	wedge
	children	hands	melts	split	when
	chunk	happen	neck	spot	with
	chunks	happened	need	standing	words
	cliffs	happening	next	steep	